IMAGES OF ENGLAND

BEACONSFIELD

STATION PARADE BEACONSFIELD

T & F. FROUDE.

R.G. WELLER. Butcher.

BEACONSFIELD STATION POST OFFICE.

BEACONSFIELD SUPPLY STORES.

SMART & NICHOLLS.

SOUTH WESTERN

FINDLOW & CO., WYCOMBE

IMAGES OF ENGLAND

BEACONSFIELD

COLIN J. SEABRIGHT

TEMPUS

Frontispiece: Adjacent to the new railway station, this parade of shops was built soon after the coming of the railway, to serve the needs of the first residents on the rapidly developing estates of the new town.

First published 2003

Tempus Publishing Limited
The Mill, Brimscombe Port,
Stroud, Gloucestershire, GL5 2QG

British Library Cataloguing in Publication Data.
A catalogue record for this book is available from the British Library.

ISBN 0 7524 3093 9

Typesetting and origination by Tempus Publishing Limited
Printed in Great Britain by Midway Colour Print, Wiltshire

Contents

Acknowledgements

All pictures are taken from postcards and photographs in my own collection. I must express my gratitude to the anonymous photographers who took the originals. Thanks are also due to the visitors and residents who first bought the postcards and sent them to friends and relations, and to those who eventually saved them in their own collections, and, unknowingly, for posterity. Thanks are also due to the writers of travel books and guides whose descriptions and opinions have been quoted in the text. I believe the copyright on all the early pictures in this volume to have expired, but the position is uncertain for those of more recent origin, and I apologise here to any copyright owners who have not been consulted; any such omissions will be acknowledged in subsequent editions.

Around the turn of the twentieth century, before the railway reached Beaconsfield, many visitors would have arrived on the Great Western Railway bus from Slough, where it connected with the London trains. On this card, published by the Railway Company, the crew posed with an almost empty bus on the crest of the hill approaching Beaconsfield, after passing Burnham Beeches en route.

Introduction

The early history of Beaconsfield mostly concerns the large estates surrounding the old town; Wilton Park, Gregories (later Butler's Court), and Hall Barn, and the influential or wealthy families who bought and sold them as their circumstances changed. The interaction between these families is too complex to detail here, but can be read in history books, particularly in the publications of the Beaconsfield and District Historical Society.

For a brief description of the town early in the nineteenth century, it is hard to improve on that in the 1830 county directory:

> Beaconsfield, a small market town in the hundred of Burnham, is twenty-three miles from London, eight from Marlow, and five from High Wycombe; pleasantly situated on a hill, and reckoned one of the most healthy situations in the kingdom. The town has many well-built houses; and there are four streets disposed in the form of a cross; these are wide and clean; the principal one is formed by the road leading from London to Oxford, and is more than half a mile in length. This town was once of considerable importance in the grain and meal trades, and its market the resort of numerous opulent factors and dealers; but the neighbouring towns of Wycombe and Uxbridge have drawn away a great portion of its business, and invaded its prosperity to a great extent; its lace-trade too, which is the only manufacture here, is in a most depressed state. Still the inhabitants are respectable, and its local trade well sustained by them in conjunction with the numerous genteel residences in the vicinage of the town.

A guide to *The Chalfont Country* described the atmosphere of the town just before the arrival of the railway:

> Beaconsfield is well worthy of a visit, for it is typical of the old country town of a century ago, through which our forefathers passed as they travelled by coach from one part of the country to another. The atmosphere of the coaching days seems to cling very closely to its fine old hostelries, and as one stands in the broad thoroughfare in front of the Royal Saracen's Head or the White Hart, it does not require much effort of the imagination to picture the arrival of the London and Oxford coach, and the animated scene as the horses were changed, and guard and coachman told to an admiring ring of stablemen and rustics the latest news from the city.

The stagecoach had brought prosperity to Beaconsfield; situated on the main London to Oxford road, a day's journey from each, it had been the obvious overnight stop for the coaches, and the town's many inns catered for this trade, providing fresh horses for the coaches and accommodation for their passengers. The railway age ended that business for Beaconsfield, which, initially bypassed by the main lines, failed to gain any benefit from the early railways. It was not until 1906 that the last new line to be built into London brought a railway service to Beaconsfield, with a station nearly a mile to the north of the old town. This station became the nucleus of a separate community, and the New Town then expanded in all directions, soon becoming a continuous conurbation with the old. In 1910, a guide to *Where to Live Round London* described the town thus:

The old town of Beaconsfield keeps its quiet and picturesque aspect in sturdy defiance of the railways, but the outlying districts, especially on the north, are rapidly changing. Many new houses have been and are being built here, most of them near the railway station. This is about three-quarters of a mile from the old town, but an omnibus meets the trains. The name of Beaconsfield attained worldwide celebrity about thirty years ago, when it gave the title of Earl to Benjamin Disraeli. But the place has had other associations with famous men, for here, in the seventeenth century, lived Edmund Waller, more creditably known as a poet than a statesman, though he had some claim to both titles. Here too, in the eighteenth century, lived Edmund Burke. The whole of the country estate of this great statesman and orator has been sold, and is being developed as a residential estate, but the old grounds have not thereby fallen into desecrating hands. The grove in which the famous orator used to stroll with many of the noted men of his day is no longer quite hidden from the world, but a great portion of the trees are still standing, while, as the new houses have each an acre or so of ground, many of the views are kept. Apart from its historic associations, the old town is in itself very attractive, on account of its beauty, its peacefulness, and the generous width of its main streets.

Then, in 1920, the author of a county book had this to say of Beaconsfield:

Of late years, since the advent of the railway, its pavements have been brightened by the appearance of smartly-dressed residents from the new suburb which has sprung up on the north of the old town and around the railway station; a place of artistic villas set widely apart, reaching along the roads towards Amersham and Penn, thus making a recently remote country semi-suburban in character....

The old town survived the early twentieth century almost untouched thanks to the neighbouring new town, where all modern development took place, and in 1930 a guide described old Beaconsfield as 'a typical eighteenth-century village on the Oxford Road with wide tree-lined side-walks and broad cross-roads', and new Beaconsfield as 'a suburb of the very best quality which has grown up round the station'.

Also in the thirties, a guide to the Wycombe area has this to say of the town as a whole:

Modern Beaconsfield enjoys all the advantages of a country district, coupled with up-to-date conveniences. There are flourishing amateur dramatic and musical societies, and excellent cricket and golf clubs, both the latter in Wilton Park, and the golf club enjoys the additional advantage of a station, Seer Green, just at the club house. A fine new church has been built to serve the needs of the new town and Knotty Green. The place is entirely residential and agricultural, though an up-to-date film studio has been built north of the old town. For the sightseer and tourist, the town has equal attractions. Its broad main street is one of the most picturesque round about. It is bordered with trees, and tall, flat-fronted Georgian and earlier houses, many being relics of the numerous inns which flourished here in the coaching days.

Thanks to enlightened planners, this description still holds true and the majority of the pictured scenes are still recognisable today.

The pictures in this book, mostly postcards dating from the first half of the twentieth century, are arranged in a geographical sequence, starting with the London to Oxford Road, then following the Windsor to Aylesbury Road through both old and new towns, with occasional detours to include places of interest off the main route. Postcards when posted occasionally picked up smudge marks from wet postmarks on adjacent items of post, and a few of the cards used in this volume have suffered in this way; however the marks usually appear in the sky area of a picture and hopefully do not detract from its detail.

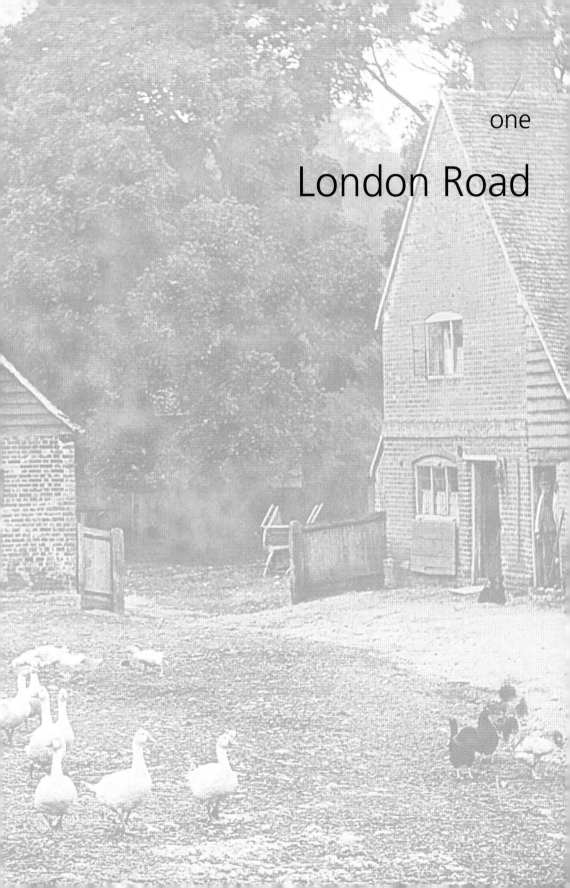

one

London Road

Until superseded recently by the M40 passing to its south, the main road from London to Oxford ran through the centre of Old Beaconsfield, and, particularly during the stagecoach era, brought prosperity to the town, situated as it was roughly halfway between the two cities. Since the mid-thirties, the first sight of Beaconsfield after the open country from Gerrards Cross has been the Bell House Hotel, photographed here soon after it opened. Judging by the hundred or so vehicles in its car park alongside the trunk road, it was already very popular with passing motorists.

One of the main attractions of the Bell House was its open-air swimming pool at the edge of the hotel complex, surrounded by a ring of curtained changing cubicles, which screened the pool from the adjoining countryside. Seen here in the thirties, the tables and chairs round the edge of the pool appear even more popular than the pool itself, although quite a few people are sitting on the edge with their toes in the water.

Half a mile nearer Beaconsfield, at a point known as Sandy Bottom, a side turning from the A40 leads directly to the Quaker centre at Jordans. At the same junction is the back gate of the Wilton Park Estate, which adjoins the road for the remaining mile and a half into town. In this 1953 photograph, taken from the side turning by a member of the Greenford Cycling Club, three of his colleagues head for home along the main road on a very wet day.

On a slight eminence in the middle of its thousand-acre parkland, the front of Wilton Park Mansion was photographed here in about 1925. Formerly known as Whiltones or Wheltones Manor, after the family who lived there in the thirteenth century, it was, from 1770, the seat of the du Pre family. The estate was taken over by the military authorities during the Second World War, and the War Department subsequently demolished the mansion in 1967, replacing it with a range of nondescript buildings in the grounds.

This postcard picture of a typically English farmyard, with its 'free-range' ducks and chickens, was sent by a new employee of the Wilton Park Estate in 1906, with a note saying, 'this is the home farm here'.

Here, in 1905, the house and garden staff gather outside the gates of Wilton Park, which open onto the junction of London Road and London End. The gates have been decorated with evergreen garlands and banners, announcing, 'Welcome to Sir John Aird and Family, Wilton Park', on their arrival to take up temporary residence there.

From the same corner, Park Lane – the beginning of the main road to Amersham – marks the eastern limit of Beaconsfield's residential development with the fields of Wilton Farm and the grounds of Wilton Park on the other side. The picture dates from about 1925, when the left corner was occupied by a large house called Crossways.

two

London End

Above: This was the view in about 1930 along London End from the Wilton Park Gates, with the main road entering from the left and the Amersham Road, which had recently been given a 'B' classification under the Ministry of Transport's new main road numbering scheme, to the right. Behind and to the right of the signpost is the 400-year-old farmhouse of Bull Farm, which doubled as an inn.

Left: Pictured just before the First World War, the first shop in London End was then Ottaway's off-licence. Behind the shop was the old windmill, which was then already partly derelict.

Above and below: Between the garage and the Swan, one of the many old houses was known as 'The Old House', although, at 250 years old, it was much younger than many of its neighbours. For the latter part of the nineteenth century it had housed Arthur Denman's boy's school, listed in 1877 as a 'middle class boarding school,' and in 1883 as a 'school for the sons of gentlemen'. The International Tea Company opened their store here from about 1905, but moved to the New Town less than twenty years later. After that, Reuben Suckling opened refreshment rooms, taken over in the early thirties by Ethel Wiltshire to become 'The Old House Tea Rooms'. The upper picture shows the restaurant's newly installed bay windows, and the lower picture shows the sheltered tea gardens at the rear.

Opposite below: This view back toward Wilton Park Gates was published in 1910. To the left, the Bull Inn had been refronted in the eighteenth century, and divided into three houses. On the other side of the road is the gabled Tudor building of the Swan Inn. Beyond the inn, The London End Forge had been brought up to date, now advertising motor repairs. A few years later it was turned into a wartime munitions factory, then after the war, it became Beaconsfield Motor Company.

Beyond the Bull was another former hostelry, The Chequers Inn, taken over as the Parish Poor House in 1768. The central portion with the lower roof had then been added to increase the accommodation. George Smyth Gower, agricultural implement maker and engineer, used the building from 1863 until 1895, when he moved to Wycombe End, and his sign can be seen above the open doorway in this 1890 photograph.

Photographed in 1904, the front portion of the old Poor House had been rebuilt four years earlier as a three-bayed Victorian House, but one of the original dormitory buildings was retained behind it. In 1910 it became a children's convalescent home, which stayed there until moving to new premises at the edge of New Town. From then until the Second World War, Richard Miller, a saddler, occupied the left half, and Edwin Mills, builder, the right.

The convalescent home opened with six children, who came from the Great Ormond Street Hospital for Sick Children. Two local ladies had founded the charity, so that London children could have the benefit of a country life to speed up their complete recovery. This card dates from after the home's 1913 extension, which had increased the number of beds and cots to eleven. Their 1921 move to Station Road gave the home a much larger building and extensive grounds.

Further along the road, this distinctive three-storey building housed Morford's Stores, pictured in 1902, with the smartly aproned staff outside. Established in 1851, initially as both wholesale and retail grocers, the archway led to extensive storage buildings and stabling for their delivery horses. It remained a family business with the original telephone number, Beaconsfield 4, until the middle of the twentieth century.

Left: Returning to the south side of London End, this was the home of James Harris, a 'practical' chimney sweep, pictured in about 1920. His wife sold tobacco, confectionery and picture postcards from their front room and ran a 'cyclist's rest' refreshment room at the back. The sweeps business had been established in 1870 and James had taken over from his father, George Harris, before the end of the century, also offering a chair repair and re-caning service as a sideline.

Below: By the Second World War, the refreshment room and shop had reverted to domestic use, seen behind the lamp-post in this 1940 view. The main block of six shops, which had been created from four old cottages many years earlier, included, in the centre, a hand-loom weaving workshop, established in the early thirties. At the edge of the picture is one of a block of three seventeenth-century cottages, which have remained in residential use.

Right: Back on the north side, we come to the house known as 'The Yews'. Previously a large private house, in the thirties it was used as a nursing home, which moved to the New Town just before the war. The building, now called Cannon House, has recently been spoilt by the application of artificial painted 'pointing' in rigid lines, bearing no relation to the actual brickwork.

Below: The nursing home known as The Yews advertised facilities for medical, surgical and maternity cases, including massage and 'electrical treatment'. It also featured 'a lovely old–world garden of three acres for convalescents'. Both this card, showing part of the garden and the back of the house, and the previous card of the front, were published in about 1935.

Slightly further along, this view towards the crossroads and into Wycombe End was published in the twenties. Many of the buildings are hidden by the trees, which are a particular feature of this part of London End, growing in the wide verge between the roadway and the shops. Among the hidden buildings, Kings Head House and the adjoining Highway House were once, together, 'The Kings Head', an inn which started trading 500 years ago.

In the same part of London End, a London-bound Green Line Coach waits at the bus stop in the mid-fifties. The shelter is of the standard country bus design, made entirely of wood, including the roof shingles, and the bus is one of the RF class, first introduced in 1951.

Looking back along the same part of the road in about 1960, this card shows the trees in all their summer glory. The bus stop is still in the same place, although the shelter had been removed. Half of the old Kings Head can be seen to the left of the first tree, with its old coach arch at the edge of the picture.

On the south side again, this 1903 view is dominated by Wendover House, where the eighteenth-century façade and the Victorian bay window hide a timber-framed structure probably 200 years older still. To the left of Wendover House, behind the lamp-post, is Louis Brown's antique furniture shop, which, in the thirties, was patronised by Queen Mary.

The white façade in the centre of this 1910 view hides the timbered Crown Inn, first documented in 1510 and believed to have been used as a base by the celebrated highwayman Claude Duval. It was later divided into two properties, Burke House to the left and Burke Lodge to the right of the former coach arch.

Next to the former Crown is The Old Post House, which in the first half of Victoria's reign had been the curate's home, and the town's post and telegraph office in the late Victorian era, under postmaster Robert Henry Robens, succeeded by Miss Harriette Robens. This card, posted in 1940, also shows the recently introduced roundabout at the crossroads.

Above and below: These two pictures show sections of a charity procession through Beaconsfield in August 1911. The parade is led by the town's horse-drawn fire engine which, when it reached a fire, required all hands to the pump, employing up to twenty-six volunteers. This engine remained in service until the first motor engine, purchased by public subscription, replaced it in the early twenties.

Above and below: Just to the right of the previous pictures, Puffins Tea Shop, a 'licensed restaurant in original sixteenth-century surroundings', was a popular meeting place for morning coffee, lunch, or afternoon tea for nearly fifty years from the mid-thirties. The premises had, since the turn of the century, belonged to a plumber and decorator, and, when taken over by Puffins, were given a new but old style frontage, with a wide bay window. The two pictures, both dating from about 1938, show the exterior, and the heavily timbered interior with its massive open fireplace.

Above: On the corner of Windsor End is the most famous and the oldest of Beaconsfield's many historic inns, The Royal Saracen's Head, which is said to have been given the prefix 'Royal' by Richard Coeur-de-Lion in 1194. In the stagecoach era, it was the main place where horses were changed, but when photographed in the late thirties, it was catering for modern travellers, whose cars occupied the wide verge of London End.

Right: This photograph, taken in the late forties and printed from a damaged negative, shows part of the inn's frontage in more detail. The fake timbering had been added to the previously bare brick walls during a late Victorian restoration of the building, creating a 'Brewer's Tudor' external appearance, but the inside contains many genuine timbers.

In this late thirties view across the main crossroads, there is little sign of the traffic that would shortly necessitate a roundabout there. People could sit peacefully watching the empty roads from a seat on the corner. On the far side, the central shops of London End included three food stores with sunblinds to protect their window displays; these were, from left to right: Kings, a family butchers established in the previous century, the new 'Bon-Bon' confectionery shop, and another old family business, Vere's fish shop.

High Class Fishmonger
Ice   Merchant   and
::   Game Dealer   ::

∞

Fresh   Supplies   Daily
The   Old   Establshed
——— Business ———
Telephone No. 56
Families Waited on Daily

7   London   End,   BEACONSFIELD

Between them, George Vere senior and his son, also George, sold fish here for over sixty years from about 1904, following the Stevens family, who started the business many years before that. This was their advertisement in the 1926 edition of the Beaconsfield town guide, showing their Christmas display of game hanging outside the shop front. The shop is still in the fish trade to this day, but now of the fried variety.

Before the railway reached Beaconsfield, The Great Western Railway operated a motor-bus service from the town to Slough station in connection with their trains from there to London. In this 1905 photograph of the crossroads, one of their buses is waiting outside No.1 London End. The conductor is on his way down the open stairs after collecting fares on the top deck, which was obviously more popular than travelling inside. This service ceased after the station opened in the new town, but a local carrier then started a horse-drawn bus service to connect the old and new towns, which continued until about 1915.

This postcard view back into London End, published in about 1912, uses the name High Street, often given to the central part of both London End and Wycombe End. Its central feature is a miniature island protecting a solitary gas-lamp at the crossroads. According to some early writers, this was the widest High Street in the country, and this view gives the impression that they could have been correct.

This final view of London End, published in about 1940, looks past the last few shops (including Veres, with the sunblind) and across the full-size island into Wycombe End. Beyond the island, which still carries a central street lamp, a group of mature trees hides most of the buildings on one side of the road.

three

Wycombe End

This first view of Wycombe End was photographed in the thirties from the Saracen's Head corner. Beyond the war memorial, in the middle of Windsor End, a telephone box and a large display of timetables and other notices now accompany the seat visible in this picture on the Wycombe End corner. On the extreme right is the back of a Thames Valley bus, on the recently introduced Route 502 from West and High Wycombe to Gerrards Cross and Uxbridge. Behind the bus is the island block, formerly Day's Stores, strictly in Market Place (or Aylesbury End), and to the left of that is the start of Wycombe End.

On the south side, near the church gates, the first house of Wycombe End is of sixteenth-century, timber-framed construction, infilled with modern bricks. The end portion had been converted to house a branch of Capital and Counties Bank, later Lloyds. In this photograph, a family group poses in the open space in front of the bank after a fancy-dress parade through the town, probably in aid of a First World War charity.

Looking across Wycombe End and the open space in front of the bank and the adjacent reading room, this photograph shows the crowds gathered in 1910 to hear the proclamation of the accession of King George V, read by the chairman of the Town Council. The whole council is gathered on the balcony of the Reading Room for the occasion. The reading room, which opened in about 1890 and was open to local residents on payment of a small subscription, housed a billiards room downstairs, with the actual reading area and library above.

This postcard from the late thirties shows the main part of Wycombe End in more detail, with the trees in the grounds of Hall Place. Across the road, The George, another historic coaching inn, is flanked by two more of the town's long-established shops: to the right, Perfect's shoe repair business, and beyond the inn a news agency, which, since the First World War, had been run by Wilkinsons

The Rectory, Beaconsfield.

H. G. STONE, PHOTO

This postcard, posted in 1940, is of Hall Place, in Wycombe End. Built at the beginning of the eighteenth century, it first housed a school for boys; then from 1868 it was used as a rectory, in preference to the 'Old Rectory' in Windsor End, hence the title on the card. This was in turn superseded, after well over a hundred years, by a modern rectory, built between this one and the church.

Looking back up to The George, the open space in front of the inn and its neighbours in Wycombe End gave this area its alternative name, The Square. Despite the smart nineteenth-century brick frontage of The George, this façade hides a building of Tudor or even earlier origin, and it is known to have traded since before 1500. For years a coach staging point, in 1895 the landlord advertised 'special terms for cyclists'.

Right: This drawing of the back of
The George, published in a county
guide in 1920, shows its original
timber-framed walls and the stable-
yard. The landlord at around this time
carefully restored the interior,
removing years of wallpaper, paint
and plaster to reveal the original
structure, including a panel of wattle
and daub infilling.

Below: Almost the whole of the Old
Town is included in this 1921 aerial
view looking up Wycombe End, past
the crossroads and along London End.
This view makes the reason behind
the name 'The Square' even more
obvious. From there, Windsor End
starts at the new war memorial and,
lined with young trees, it continues
past the church. At the top of the
picture, behind the church tower, the
council's first houses in Malthouse
Square were then nearing completion.

This 1925 view back up Wycombe End to The Square shows the buildings at the bottom of the previous photograph as they were seen from ground level, including two more old public houses. On the left, the projecting bracket once held the hanging sign of The Orange Tree, and on the other side of the road, just beyond the lamp-post, The Cross Keys was still in business. At the edge of the picture the creeper-clad building was then the post office.

Another of the buildings which has, at some time, housed Beaconsfield's post office; this well-shrouded house with steps up to the door was, from about 1910 to 1930, the post and telegraph office. Pictured here in 1925, when Albert Gower was postmaster, it then also boasted a 'National Telephone Call Office'.

On the hill down from the town towards Wycombe, these cottages line the north side of Wycombe End. In between the two terraces is one of the town's younger public houses, The Prince of Wales, which opened in the middle of Victoria's reign. Behind the cottages at the top of the hill, Factory Yard was the site of two ribbon factories, which were later used as the first Church school and Wesleyan chapel early in the nineteenth century; however an adjacent Windsor Chair factory remained in operation until nearly a century later.

A little way beyond the built-up part of Wycombe End, the lodge of Butler's Court, pictured in around 1925, stood on the north side of the road beside a small pond. It was built astride the drive at about the same time as the new mansion. The lodge was demolished in the sixties to make way for a new housing estate.

The original Butler's Court, previously named Gregories after the family who owned it in the late seventeenth century, stood towards the north of its vast estate, near the present Gregories Road and with its entrance from what is now Station Road. An 1805 guide notes that, 'The grounds are tastefully laid out but not extensive'. This old drawing was reprinted in an early edition of the Beaconsfield town guide.

Gregories was bought in 1768 by Edmund Burke and was renamed Butler's Court. In 1813 it was destroyed by fire and never rebuilt. A new Butler's Court was built in 1891 much further south within the estate, with its entrance from Wycombe End. A large part of the grounds later gave way to the railway and the subsequent housing development of New Town. The house was used as a Red Cross Hospital for members of the Free French forces during the Second World War. This picture is from 1920.

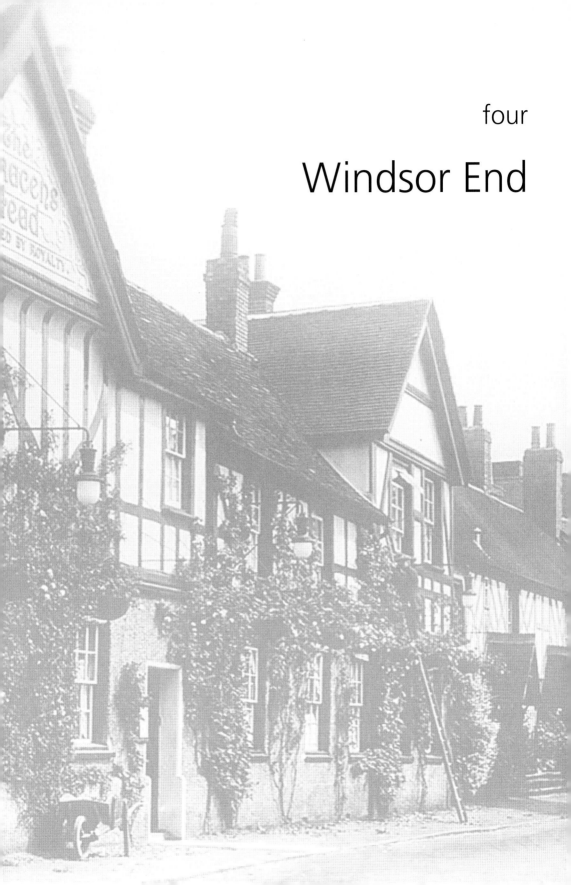

four

Windsor End

Turning now to the other arm of the crossroads, the southern approach to Beaconsfield used to be along Windsor End, but, since the construction of the M40, this has come to a dead end some half a mile from the town. For most of that length it is still bordered by the grounds of Hall Barn. Just inside the main gates of Hall Barn is a curiously decorated lodge, pictured here in about 1920.

The outside of Hall Barn Lodge is covered with ancient oak panels, all intricately carved. Most of the carvings on the upper storey were brought from Italy by Sir Gore Ousely soon after he bought the estate from the Waller family in 1844, but the lower panels, which were added over forty years later, came from a Belgian convent. More recently, any necessary replacements and repairs have been executed by local craftsmen.

This mid-twenties aerial view is of the Hall Barn parkland looking toward Beaconsfield town. In 1912 the park was noted to contain three exceptionally fine yew trees, then over 200 years old. The estate's kitchen gardens can be seen at the right edge, but The Grove, where the shooting parties often included royalty, is out of view at the bottom where the estate extended for over a mile.

Various sporting activities have taken place in the large open spaces of the grounds, and this photograph shows the mass start of the National Cross-Country Championships, held there on 9 March 1929.

Beaconsfield — Hall Barn.

Hall Barn is seen here across the lake on a 1915 postcard. The grounds, laid out for Edmund Waller in about 1650 before the house was built, have often been made available as a beautiful setting for open-air theatrical performances. A 1919 guide notes that the garden, 'is one of the few remaining examples of the style of landscape gardening which was so fashionable in England during the seventeenth century', and 'the grotto is where the poet used to sit in the garden he designed.'

A postcard dating from 1900 here shows the main north front of Hall Barn, facing the entrance drive. The left-hand three bays were a nineteenth-century addition to the original seventeenth-century building. This and other extensions were demolished in about 1970 to restore the house to its original state and a more manageable size.

This 1905 card, showing the south front of Hall Barn, was sent by a member of staff, apologising to his mother that he, 'would not be able to get home till next week as his lordship would be there for a weekend party'. The south wing was an early eighteenth-century addition to the original building, facing the lawn that runs down to the lake, which was well stocked with fish.

Photographed at the same time, this card shows the domestic offices, which had been added as part of the same extension. As well as the house staff, Hall Barn employed an army of gardeners, totalling more than twenty-five men even after the First World War.

Hall Barn Fire Brigade. Lord Burnham's Country Seat.

In addition to the domestic and garden staff, Hall Barn employed its own fire brigade, pictured here in about 1902. The men did not live on site but were roused from their homes in the town by a 'knocker-up', when required for duty. The private brigade was disbanded in about 1930, when the town brigade, with its new motor-driven fire engine, was considered adequate to cope with any emergency at the house.

At the northern edge of the park, the seventeenth-century dower house, Little Hall Barn, stands adjacent to Windsor End. Pictured just after the First World War, its construction, entirely of purple and red brick, had earned it the alternative title 'The Brick Place'.

Windsor End narrowed suddenly where it squeezed between the Hall Barn staff cottages and Little Hall Barn, to the left and right respectively in this 1905 out-of-town view. All the pictured cottages together with a similar number including the Plough Inn further into town were demolished to allow for road widening in 1956, a sacrifice now rendered completely unnecessary by the post-motorway diversion of through traffic.

Further into Beaconsfield, again looking south, in about 1910, the entrance to the narrow section of Windsor End is in the centre of the picture beside the square house on the corner of Hedgerley Lane. Built in 1900, this was the old school headmaster's residence, also demolished for road widening. At the extreme left is the ancient pub, The Greyhound, originally called 'Ye Greyhound Dogge' and sometimes referred to as simply The Dog.

Continuing to the left of the previous view this 1900 photograph includes, in the centre, the late Victorian police station, then manned by an inspector and two constables. It was built in 1872, incorporating the inspector's residence, and boasted a 'county' shield over the door, some seventy years before the arms were officially granted.

Behind the houses on the left of the previous two cards, Malthouse Square, pictured in 1925, was the first modern housing development in the old town. Beaconsfield Council started this scheme in 1919, building fifty-two 'parlour-type' homes there around a central green.

MALTHOUSE SQUARE, BEACONSFIELD.

Included in this 1930 view of Malthouse Square is the stump of the old windmill situated just off London End. Built in 1811 of brick and flint rendered with cement, the octagonal tower still stood, but without its cap. It had fallen into disuse in 1880, and after that the sails and machinery gradually disappeared. The tower itself finally collapsed in 1974.

Old Beaconsfield from the Air.

Photographed from above Hall Barn in 1922, this aerial view shows the wide part of Windsor End, with its narrow bottleneck at the bottom corner. The police station can be picked out to the right of the first tree of the line along the road. Further fully-grown trees hide the graveyard and part of the church and adjacent Old Rectory. The white building at the top centre of the picture is the newly opened film studio off Station Road and to the right of that is the new housing development along Candlemas Lane, beyond which, almost as far as the railway cutting, was still open country.

Looking at the west side of the street, the most prominent feature is the three mature elm trees, each with its surrounding rustic seat. These remained a part of Windsor End's scenery until they were lost to Dutch Elm Disease. Another tree that attracts attention is the topiary in the first garden, next to the drive to the Old Rectory, not looking its usual neatly trimmed best when photographed some time in the fifties.

The footway on the west side continues into town as a path between the churchyard fence and a post and chain barrier beside The Green. This photograph, looking across The Green to the Windsor End shops, was taken on a winter's day in 1907; there are hardly any signs of life visible either there or at the crossroads.

Opposite below: Returning to the east side of Windsor End, the first shop we come to is the bakery. There had been bakers by the name of Blake in Beaconsfield since 1880, but this 1908 postcard shows their new 'Church Side Model Bakery', which had taken the place of an old cottage on the site, and was to continue in business until after the Second World War.

Taking a closer look at the line of shops, this 1940 postcard includes another home of Beaconsfield's wandering post office, then only a sub-office since the new head office opened near the station. It stayed here for thirty years, from about 1930. To the right of the post office, hidden by the tree, was the Chester House Tea Rooms, with Blake's bakery beyond that.

All Windsor End's shops are in mock-Tudor style, similar to the Saracens Head, the side of which completes their line up to the crossroads. Pictured in about 1925, the stark lines of the inn's timbering were then softened by a few trees fan-trained over the surface, one of which a workman is busy securing to the first floor 'timbering'.

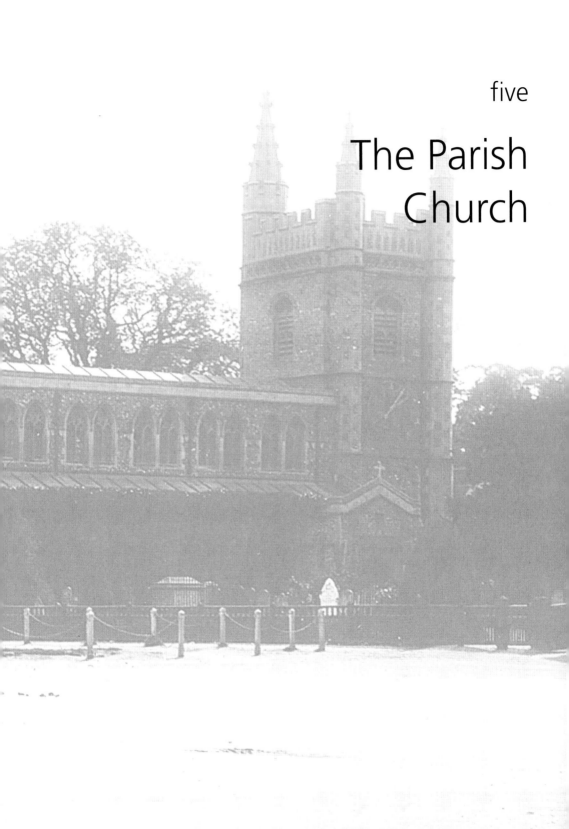

five

The Parish
Church

The churchyard lines the west side of Windsor End facing the shops. This 1910 view across the green and the graveyard with its selection of trees includes the Old Rectory and, almost hidden to the right, the church itself. The group of children are probably on their way to or from the church school, out of sight to the left, which was built in 1872 on the site of the old tithe barn.

Opposite, above and below: Standing on the site of a nunnery associated with Burnham Abbey, the Old Rectory was built early in the sixteenth century and used as such until the Rector's move to Hall Place in 1868. After that it was allowed to fall into decay so much that an 1897 guide refers to the 'picturesque remains' of the old building. The upper picture shows the derelict state of the front walls at about that date, with broken infilling between the massive timbers of the frame. It was restored both inside and out in 1901 by Lord Burnham of Hall Barn in memory of his late wife, and subsequently well maintained partly for parish offices and partly as the Beaconsfield Free Library; the lower picture was taken in June 1938 from the neatly turfed graveyard.

Above: In this winter scene from about 1925 the church is seen across Windsor End and The Green, where John Hampden, a local parliamentary in the English Civil War, is said to have drilled a group of volunteers to fight for his cause, and which later became the playground for the nearby church school. Just to the right of the tree in the church grounds is the pointed obelisk on the tomb of Edmund Waller, who had spent his later years at Hall Barn.

Left: Situated under a great walnut tree, this being the crest of the Waller family, the immense marble tomb of Edmund Waller, who died in 1687, is the most prominent monument in the churchyard. The white marble base, engraved on all sides with Latin texts, is covered with a carved pall of black marble, all surmounted by a tall obelisk resting on four skulls. A 1926 guide described the tomb as, 'a deplorably ugly erection in the worst style of its period'.

Above: Photographed in the fifties, when Waller's walnut tree was dying of old age, this card shows the south side of the parish church. Built mostly in the fifteenth century, it was 'restored' in 1869, and the author of a guide book in the twenties noted that it was 'almost rebuilt by the frenzied zeal of nineteenth-century restorers', but another in 1937 described it as 'a splendid church which the nineteenth century did not spoil'.

Right: The south porch of the church, erroneously described as north on this 1917 postcard, was added in memory of the rector who had been responsible for the 1869 restoration. The roof of the porch was made from the timbers of the old bell-cage when it was renovated as part of the 1884 rebuild of the tower.

North Porch.
Beaconsfield.Church.
WHA 2028

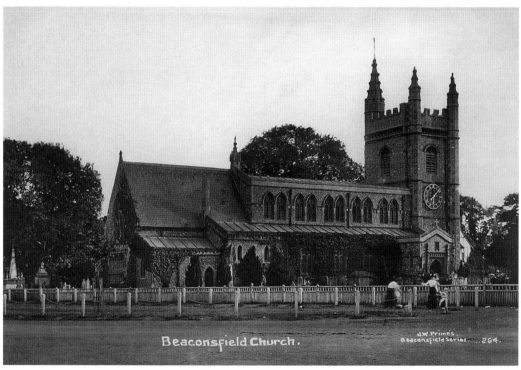

Beaconsfield Church.

J.W.Prime's
Beaconsfield Series. 264.

This is the handsome interior, described as 'impressive in a sombre way', as the Victorians left it, pictured in the early years of the twentieth century. Although much of the structure had been rebuilt it still included many of the original fitments, such as old brasses and memorials and including one to Edmund Burke, whose private pew had been rebuilt as a cabinet for books and music, and part of a fifteenth-century carved screen.

Opposite above: Published as a postcard roughly a hundred years later, this old drawing portrays the north side of the church in 1802, well before the Victorians started work on it. Described in a contemporary guide as being 'composed of flint and square stones', with the inside 'neatly plaistered and white-washed', it then featured a wooden spire with only a low balustrade round the top of the tower.

Opposite below: Pictured from the same viewpoint in about 1915, this card shows the external changes wrought by the restorers. The church was lengthened and the roof rebuilt with extended clerestory in 1869, and the tower given battlements and corner pinnacles fifteen years later, together with a clock 'erected by subscription and set agoing on the fifteenth day of May in the year of Our Lord 1885'.

The church dominates the view from the crossroads on this 1913 postcard. The posts surround the top end of the green, with a further large open space in front of the churchyard and beside the old building at the corner of Wycombe End, which then housed the town's only bank.

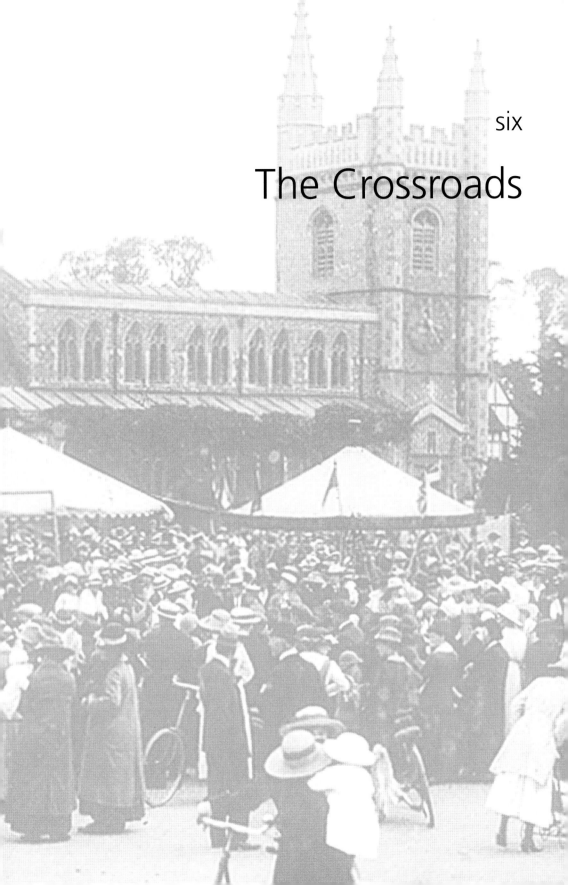

six

The Crossroads

Above: Seen from the corner of Market Place in about 1910, the width of the streets makes the area at the crossroads look vast, particularly as the open space is only broken by two objects. The signpost for the White Hart stands well away from the building at the corner of Aylesbury End, and the solitary lamp-post is in the entrance to Windsor End. This large area is the obvious place to hold the annual fair and other such gatherings.

Beaconsfield War Memorial. The Unveiling.

Reeves)

Above: This second photograph of the unveiling shows more detail of the memorial itself, with the side of the Saracens Head in the background. This type of memorial is known as a 'Lanterne aux Mortes', with the top lantern supported on an octagonal shaft with a Calvary on its north face. The names of the eighty local men who fell were carved on the panels of the square plinth.

Opposite below: In 1921 the town's memorial to those who died in the First World War replaced the lamp–post in the entrance to Windsor End. It was unveiled in May by Field Marshall Lord Grenfell of Butler's Court, whose son had been posthumously awarded the first Victoria Cross of the war, but it was not dedicated until Remembrance Day. This photograph shows the crowd at the unveiling.

The memorial's position in the carriageway, where there had previously been a street lamp, necessitated something to protect it from traffic and vice versa, so the lantern was permanently illuminated by four electric light bulbs inside. The local Girl Guides took on the task of regularly removing dead flowers and scrubbing traffic dirt from the base of the memorial.

By 1936 traffic had increased to such an extent that the memorial, even though well illuminated, had become a hazard and, despite a storm of protest, it was moved a few yards to the safety of The Green. A few years later the first of a series of different shaped roundabouts was installed at the crossroads, and this 1945 postcard shows both these changes, and the use of the area beside the bank as a bus terminus.

Beaconsfield's annual fairs on the common land of Windsor and Wycombe End were authorised by a charter of 1269 granted to Burnham Abbey, who then owned the area, and by fresh grants in 1414 and 1551. The dates seem to have varied but from about 1870 the general fair was held on 10 May, with a cattle fair on 13 February, but the latter died out thirty years later. This photograph from around 1910 shows the crowds at the May Fair.

After 1921 the fair had to fit its attractions around the War Memorial, and in this early twenties photograph, the memorial's lantern can be seen behind Gipsy Smith's fortune-telling booth and a set of swing-boats. A showman's engine is parked in Windsor End between the stalls, to which it supplies electricity.

Another view of the fair, also from the twenties but this time looking into London End, shows the road wide enough to accommodate the fair without disrupting traffic on the Oxford Road. Thirty years later, with more cars on the road and larger items of fairground equipment, severe traffic jams became a regular feature of the fair days, only relieved when the M40 diverted most of the through traffic away from the town.

Looking towards Market Place, this view of the celebrations following the May 1910 proclamation of the accession of King George V was sent by one of the brass-helmeted fireman standing immediately behind the band's trombone player to the left of the picture. He had drawn a small cross on the image of his helmet to help the recipient identify him from the rest of the crowd.

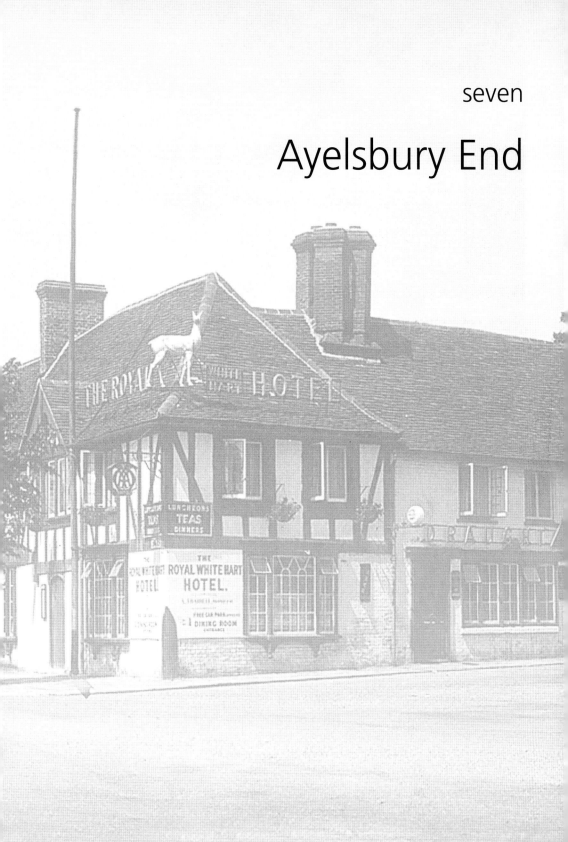

seven

Ayelsbury End

This view of Aylesbury End from the parapet of the church tower is postmarked 1914. The island block in the centre of the view, known as Market Place, was occupied by Day's Supply Stores. The block includes the remains of the original Market Hall, site of the regular charter market until its closure early in the nineteenth century. The market was revived in 1982, but is now held in the open air in Windsor End.

A postcard from the turn of the century, this shows the side of Market Place with the Day family's home, which incorporated part of the ancient market hall, at the edge of the view. Beyond it another island building in Aylesbury End, the former town lock-up, then housed another grocery firm, Spencer and Readhead.

The view into Aylesbury End, between Market Place and the White Hart, is pictured here in about 1910. Day's Stores, (grocers, drapers, clothiers and wine and spirit merchants), was prominent on the corner of Market Place, where the family had traded for fifty years.

Looking over the crossroads in a westerly direction, Market Place is on the right of the scene on this 1933 postcard. The double-fronted shop, formerly Day's, was then occupied by a greengrocer, and the shop on the other corner, which had been Blake's bakery in the early years of the century, was then The Oak Tea Rooms, with menu boards on the pavement in front of its windows.

In this 1910 view of Aylesbury End, the Royal White Hart Hotel is on the right with a group of ladies standing at its coach-yard entrance. Built in about 1600, it was one of the town's most important coaching inns, boasting stabling for 100 horses. From 1882-24 it was renamed the Manor Hotel, thought by the Victorians to be a more upmarket title.

The inn issued this card in 1931, bearing a facsimile of the landlord's signature. Since the previous view, its frontage had gained more 'Elizabethan' timbering and a model of a White Hart instead of the painted sign on the roof. The signpost, which has always been sited well away from the inn (even incurring a fine for the innkeeper in 1624 for setting it out too far from the building), then also carried direction signs.

A companion card shows part of the beamed interior of the building in 1931. The inn has welcomed a host of important people over the centuries and many of their signatures were preserved in its visitor's books. Local celebrity G.K. Chesterton was a 'regular' between the wars, and it is believed that both Queen Elizabeth I and Oliver Cromwell were among its early guests.

This GWR single-deck solid-tyred bus, standing at its terminus beside the White Hart in 1904, provided the Beaconsfield to Slough service until the introduction of double-deckers. It acted as a feeder service to connect with that company's trains between Slough and London. Although Wooburn Green station on the Bourne End to High Wycombe branch would have been a much shorter bus journey, Slough had the advantage of direct main-line trains.

Pictured here in the early thirties, the true position of the Royal White Hart can be seen more clearly, standing on the corner of Shepherds Lane, not London End. The lane starts between the white building of the inn and the darker brick building, No.1 London End, then a corn and feed merchants. Maintenance work there in the sixties revealed seventeenth-century wall paintings hidden behind countless layers of wallpaper.

Opposite above: Published in about1940, this postcard shows the Royal White Hart's Aylesbury End frontage including the new left-hand gable, added with the additional timbering, and beneath it the resited main entrance, which had previously been via the door behind the tree. To the right of the inn, one can see well into Shepherds Lane, behind the buildings of London End.

Opposite below: A little way into Aylesbury End, showing the White Hart's stable (the white building at the right edge), this 1910 photograph includes the whole of the old lock-up, originally only one storey, where vagrants and petty criminals were held overnight. Made redundant by the Victorian police station, it became a shop, then a warehouse, and from about 1930 housed the Hall Barn Estate Office.

ROYAL WHITE HART HOTEL, BEACONSFIELD

AYLESBURY END, BEACONSFIELD.

Published just before the First World War, this view further into Aylesbury End includes the 1876 Congregational church, built on the burial ground of its predecessor, which was retained further back on the same site as a Sunday school hall. At the left edge is the Old Hare, bearing a huge sign for its brewers, Salters of Rickmansworth, across the whole of its frontage.

Looking back from the edge of the Old Town, where Aylesbury End leads into Station Road, in about 1914, this short street then still included four inns and beer-houses from the ten which had been there at various times over the centuries. This card was sent by a member of staff of the newly opened Beaconsfield Sanitary Laundry, the white building with the horse and cart outside. At the edge of the view, beside the ivy-covered house, was the entrance to Mr Child's coal yard, soon to move to Station Approach in the New Town.

eight

Station Road

The northward continuation of Aylesbury End was known as Station Road after the 1906 opening of Beaconsfield station, the best part of a mile from the crossroads. Pictured here in 1910, it was still only a rough country lane despite being the direct highway between the old and new towns, but already boasted the modern convenience of street lamps fed from the gas-works, halfway along the road.

Opposite above and below: Beaconsfield's most famous resident of the twentieth century came to the town more or less by accident. But having arrived in the town, G.K. Chesterton and his wife liked what they saw and decided to settle there. In 1909 they bought Overroads (above), on the corner of Station Road and the partly developed Grove Road. A few years later his studio was built in Top Meadow, the field across the road, followed in 1922 by the house where they lived until his death in 1936. The lower picture shows the studio and house behind the garden designed for the great man by his wife.

Mrs. A. H. Chesterton's House, Beaconsfield,

Above and below: Further along Station Road the old Candlemas Lane branches off to the east, with this pond in the corner. The top picture, a 1913 postcard, shows the view across the very natural pond to Station Road, where an open carriage waits outside the newly built house opposite the lane. Below, looking the other way ten years later, the first house in Candlemas Lane can be seen over the now smartened pond, surrounded by ornamental plants, while there are still open fields on the other side of the lane most of the way to the railway cutting.

St. Joseph's Nursing Home, Beaconsfield. Front View.

Above and below: In 1936, only a month before his death, G.K. Chesterton spoke at the opening ceremony of the newly built St Joseph's Nursing Home, which the Sisters of Bon Secours had started two years earlier in the neighbouring house, 'Fernhurst', in Candlemas Lane opposite the back of the film studios. These views of St Joseph's are from a set of half a dozen postcards published shortly after it opened.

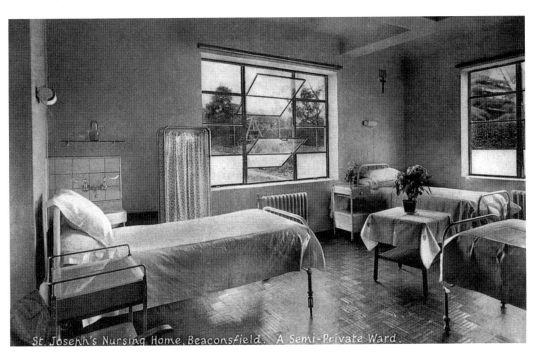

St. Joseph's Nursing Home, Beaconsfield. A Semi-Private Ward.

At the far end of Candlemas Lane where it joins Park Lane, the main Amersham road, these terraced houses, pictured in about 1910, back onto the town's cemetery at the end of Shepherds Lane.

Station Road, Beaconsfield.

J.W. Prime's
Beaconsfield Series. 1735.

Just beyond the gasworks, the only other buildings on the east side of Station Road were the house and barns of Davenies Farm, pictured here in about 1918, just before development started in earnest on its extensive fields. In 1940 the Revd Newton founded Davenies preparatory school for boys in the former farm buildings.

Opposite below: This view returns to Station Road, looking north from Candlemas Corner in about 1913; the road had been surfaced in 1911 and a pavement added to serve the new large houses built behind the line of mature trees. Just visible to the right is part of Gas Cottage, next door to the gasworks, which had been established in the 1860s.

S 15200 Station Road, Beaconsfield

The end of the residential part of Station Road is shown on this postcard published in the late twenties. Behind the trees on the right are the grounds of White Barn, which from 1921 housed the greatly expanded Children's Convalescent Home. The shopping centre then began just round the bend of the road in the distance.

nine

The New
Estates

·HOVSES
·BVRKES ESTATE·
·BEACONSFIELD·

LOW RATES.   3 MINUTES FROM STATION.
35 MINUTES' RUN TO PADDINGTON OR
.   MARYLEBONE (FREQUENT TRAINS).   .
GRAVEL SOIL.   .   .   .   .   .   .
COMPANY'S WATER AND GAS.   .   .   .

AGENTS: GURNEYS, BEACONSFIELD.

Above: Property developers invariably followed the railway builders, and soon after the opening of Beaconsfield station, large numbers of houses were built in the vicinity. The first were along the existing lanes, Station Road, Penn Road, Ledborough Lane and, nearer the old town, one side of Candlemas Lane. These were followed by the new roads of the 300 acre Burke's Estate on the former lands of Gregories House and Farm, which had been cut in two by the railway cutting. This postcard of the partly developed Burkes Road was published in about 1912.

Left: This advertisement for houses on the new Burkes Estate appeared in the 1910 issue of the guide, 'Where to Live Round London, North Side'.

A little further north, Gregories Road was another early development, beside the railway cutting and leading to Burgess Wood, which stood just within the western boundary of both the old estate and the Beaconsfield Urban District. Pictured in about 1912, the road was still only a rough track although rapidly filling with large houses.

Pictured in 1920, the forty-acre Burgess Wood initially formed a barrier to development, but by 1925 the footpaths had been replaced by roads and scattered houses were being built among the trees. A quarter of a century later the situation was reversed, with only scattered trees among the houses, and now only a couple of acres of the old woodland remain.

This aerial view shows the extent of the Burke's Estate in about 1926. Burkes Road itself runs down the middle of the view with the massed trees of Walk Wood to the right, and the railway line cuts across the top left corner. At the lower left a large gravel pit had been excavated for estate building material and below that is the edge of Burgess Wood.

At the same time as the main part of the estate, Baring Road was under development in the isolated portion north of the railway. Also parallel to the line, it was connected to Gregories Road by a footpath bridging the cutting. The Beaconsfield Baptist chapel was built in between the right-hand houses in 1915, a year after the publication of this postcard.

Above and below: At the edge of the estate, Reynolds Road was another early development linking up with Baring Road at both ends. The upper card, posted in 1914 with the sender's house indicated, shows the western end of the road. The lower, nearer the town centre, but including a large still-vacant plot, is of the same date. Part of that plot remained empty until the town's library was built there in about 1960.

Reynolds and Baring Roads continue as Woodside Road to the edge of the estate at Hogback Wood, a National Trust property which limits the town's expansion in that direction. Pictured in about 1920, only a few houses had then been built along the edge of the wood.

This closer view of one of the houses backing on to the wood was sent bearing a 1912 Christmas greeting from the lady of the house, pictured here in front of her home.

ten

New Town
Shopping
Centre

Instead of following the geographical sequence, this section illustrates the growth of the southern half of Beaconsfield's new shopping centre along Station Road, in chronological order. Development spread out from the station and the first view, published only a year or two after the opening of the railway, is of the new shops on the western side of Station Approach. There is an empty plot being offered for sale at the far end of the parade, seen here from the railway bridge. The nearest, mock-Tudor, shop was Capital & Counties Bank, a sub-branch of the establishment in the Old Town. Next to them was the office of Gurneys, agents for the new houses on the Burkes Estate.

Opposite below: Looking up Station Approach, again in about 1912, we can see over the bridge to the first parade of shops north of the railway. Also visible to the right over the bridge parapet are the huts, which housed the very first businesses beside the top of the slope, which led to the up platform.

Above: A wider view of Station Approach from the far side of the bridge in about 1912, this includes Frost's Estate Agency right on the edge of the railway cutting. Their name, together with that of High Wycombe house furnishers, Rolls, on the side of the building could be seen from a long distance until new buildings obscured the view. On the other side of the road the only building was the stationmaster's house; the remainder was lined with trees, most of which remained until well into the twenties.

As part of the gradual growth of the town centre, the foundation stone of the first Council Chambers, the offices of Beaconsfield Urban District Council, was laid in 1911. This view of the completed building on the corner of Station Road and Burkes Road was published about five years later, with the edge of the Town's Assembly Hall to the right of Burkes Road.

Postmarked 1915, this card shows the Town Hall building, where dances, plays, and other such functions were held. Adjoining the front of the hall, the two-storeyed building with the prominent bay window was then occupied by The Beaconsfield Constitutional Club. In the early thirties the premises were taken over by W.H. Smith's, and by the end of that decade Five Ways Café opened there. The annexe to the right was rebuilt with two storeys in the twenties as a shop, first occupied by a drapery.

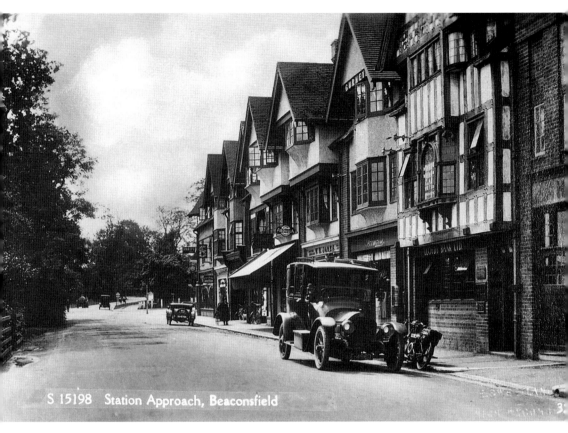

S 15198   Station Approach, Beaconsfield

This view was published in about 1924, and the first block of shops had, by then, been renamed Burkes Parade, with another shop added at the far end in a plainer style than the rest. This was occupied by Mayne's ironmongery and cycle shop, which also sold Pratt's motor spirit to the town's first motorists.

This 1925 card of the view towards the bridge includes the frontage of Mayne's store, which had spread into the timbered premises on the sharp corner of Gregories Road. In the middle of Burkes Parade, Batte's fishmongers is well protected by sunblinds in the premises they were to occupy for half a century. On the other side of the road the trees were still there, but not for much longer.

Looking in the same direction again in 1930 from further back along Station Road; a new block of shops named The Highway had been built on the east side with the new head post office at the far end facing Burkes Parade. A photographer now used the upper storey of Mayne's shop, and beside it new shops were open in Gregories Road.

Pictured in 1932, every shop in the first block of The Highway had its sunblinds extended, protecting window displays from the afternoon sun. On the corner of Maxwell Road (right), W.H. Smith's new shop was fitted out with their then familiar frontage, and a full window display.

The new Picture House, with its distinctive arched entrance, opened in 1927, and the shops facing it, the second parade of The Highway, opened in 1933. Then, after the Urban District Council offices moved to their new premises beyond the station in 1936, their old building was extended with shops fronting both Burkes Road and Station Road along to the cinema, as seen on this late thirties postcard.

On some unspecified occasion in the early forties, probably a money-raising event for war weapons, a bugle corps and band lead a military parade past the Picture House and neighbouring shops, where a good crowd of onlookers has gathered. Next door to the cinema is the Saracen Bookshop, then the decorated premises of Country Clothes, with the entrance to the upstairs Burkes Court in between.

A postcard from the late forties, this shows the completed Highway, then filled with local independent traders, with Boots and Smiths the being only multiples. It also indicates the complex five-way junction, from which the tea room took its name, and which today is managed by three mini-roundabouts. Branching from the main Station Road, Maxwell Road runs to the left beside Smiths, with Gregories and Burkes Roads both to the right, respectively before and beyond the tea room.

Above and below: These two cards published in the forties show mostly familiar aspects of the shopping centre, though there have been some major alterations and many of the shops have changed hands since then. In the top picture, the stationmaster's house, whose garden then still reached the edge of the road facing Burkes Parade, was replaced in the fifties by a supermarket. In the lower view can be seen the Five Ways Tea Room and the old Town Hall behind it, which were demolished in the sixties and replaced by a block of flats.

When the new purpose-built Picture House opened just down the road, the Town Hall closed as a cinema and reverted to its former use, holding various functions including dances on its perfectly sprung floor. This picture is of an unusual and rather more mundane activity being held there, with post office staff sorting the mail at 4.30 a.m. during the Christmas rush in 1954.

Pictured in the sixties from the wide pavement in front of the new block on the corner between Burkes and Gregories Roads, this view includes the post office building (behind the lamp-post) and, beyond it, the supermarket which replaced the stationmaster's house.

eleven

The Railway

Above: Posted only five days after the opening of the Great Western and Great Central Joint Railway through Beaconsfield, this scene must have been photographed just before completion of the station. The last new main line into London, the railway was built to a high standard, with four tracks through the stations to allow expresses on the inner tracks to overtake local trains at the platforms.

Another photograph from very soon after the opening, the new station is seen here from the up platform, with a local train to High Wycombe on the other side. At this stage no buildings can be seen on Station Road, which crosses the tracks on the arched brick bridge beyond the station footbridge.

Opposite below: Photographed from the top of the main approach on the north side of the tracks shortly after the opening, this view gives an idea of the extent of the excavation needed to accommodate the station. In addition to the station buildings and platforms, space was used further along the northern approach for a goods yard with sidings and a depot building, all well below the natural ground level.

Beaconsfield Station.

Looking across the station from the top of the embankment, the misty outline of Station Parade can be seen over the footbridge on this 1910 postcard. Further to the right is the Railway Hotel and beyond that the first of the residential buildings north of the railway.

Opposite above and below: These photographs, were both taken on 21 August 1920, when the Great Central were running thirty local trains to Marylebone and the Great Western seven to Paddington every day. The top view, from the middle of the road bridge, is of a down local at the platform, and also includes the post office depot at the top of the embankment, and the two approach slopes, one to each platform. The lower view, from part way down the north slope, shows a Birmingham express hauled by 'Saint Sebastian' racing through the station on the fast line.

Pictured from track level in September 1936, a down Great Western express, drawn by locomotive 5018, steams along between Beaconsfield's goods depot and the signal box before passing through the station on its way to the midlands.

This view of a London-bound commuter train pulling into the platform dates from the early sixties, before the fast lines were lifted as an economy measure. The roof of the main post office is visible over the awning of the down platform.

twelve

New Town Shops
(continued)

Beaconsfield's shopping centre continues north of the railway, including the very first shops of the new town, temporary buildings in Penn Road at the top of the slope from the north side of the station. One of these was photographed some ten years later, hard up against the bridge parapet. It faced a group of smaller huts on the other side of the station path, which also served the needs of the new residents. The pictured hut was the greengrocer's shop of Thomas Griffin of Wycombe End, whose wife advertised in the shop window as teacher of music. The hut's end panel and part of the roof were let out as advertising space for other local firms from the old town.

Looking north from the railway bridge in 1908, this was the start of the new shopping centre, which, as on the other side of the railway, would then grow outward from the station. The first houses of Reynolds Road can be seen beyond Station Parade, while a horse-drawn delivery cart waits near one of the temporary shops beside the station path.

Facing Station Parade and only 100 yards from the station, the Railway Hotel, 'the only modern hotel in the district', opened immediately after the railway and was photographed within its first year. Despite its modern facilities it still catered for horses as well as cars, offering livery and bait stables, loose boxes and stabling for hunters, carriages and brakes to order, and a motor garage. Later, when no longer required for horse-drawn traffic the stabling became the base for a riding school.

Another photograph from 1910, this shows two of the new shops in Station Parade in detail. Beaconsfield Station Post Office, newsagent, bookseller, stationer, tobacconist, confectioner, toys and fancy goods dealer, also offered a library service (in connection with W.H. Smith) and sold seeds, manures, fertilizers and garden requisites, with a delivery service throughout the district. Next door, Beaconsfield Supply Stores, high-class family grocer and provision merchant, stockists of 'Italian goods' and tin and ironware, advertised 'families waited on daily'.

Postmarked 1911, this card shows the whole of Station Parade, which by then could supply all the everyday needs of the new residents. The shops at that date were, from left to right: No. 1, temporarily closed, refitting as an art-needlework shop; No. 2, William Poole, fruiterer; No. 3, Rupert Weller, butcher; No. 4, S.A. Holland's, Beaconsfield station post office; No. 5, Samuel Thorp, Beaconsfield Supply Stores; No. 6, Joseph Nicholls, fancy draper. No. 7, London and South Western Bank Ltd, was a full-time branch, which was also responsible for a part-time sub-branch at Gerrards Cross, only open on Tuesdays and Fridays.

Opposite below: Rupert Weller's butchers shop remained in Station Parade from the completion of the building until the Second World War. This picture of a very full window display appeared in his advertisement in the town guide in the twenties.

Above: Looking the other way down Station Parade, this card, bearing a 1914 postmark, shows Nos. 3-7, and the panelled side of No. 1 and 2, which are set much further forward. The bank premises extended round the domed corner into Baring Road.

Looking back from further along Penn Road in 1920, a pavement was then under construction past the Railway Hotel, while trees had grown up on the opposite site where Westminster Bank would shortly be built, facing the old bank, by then taken over by Barclays.

Another north view a few years later; this includes the new Westminster Bank, set well back from Penn Road, allowing the old tree to remain beside the road. On the other side the shrubs and trees in front of the Railway Hotel and on the spare ground between it and the railway cutting have grown well and almost hide the next block of shops.

EARL OF BEACONSFIELD.

From its initial opening, the Railway Hotel was managed by Mr and Mrs Borlase, devout Catholics who, from 1914, offered the assembly room behind the hotel for use as a temporary Catholic church. The altar was positioned in a corner, where it could easily be hidden by curtains when the hall was needed for other purposes. It was in this hall in 1922 that Gilbert Keith Chesterton was received into the Catholic faith by Father O'Connor, later immortalised as the Father Brown of G.K. Chesterton's stories. After the deaths of Mr and Mrs Borlase, new landlords took over the hotel in the early thirties and renamed it The Earl of Beaconsfield.

The new headquarters building for the Beaconsfield Urban District Council was opened in 1936 on the open space beside the Railway Hotel. The impressive building, set back from the road behind a well-kept area of grass known as Council Green, was photographed the following year.

Looking north from the station path past the council chamber in about 1960; decorative flowerbeds surround the council green. Beyond, a portrait of Disraeli appears on the sign for the Earl of Beaconsfield Hotel, which was demolished some twenty years later to make way for a supermarket. On the other side of the road the spare ground between the two banks was then being used as an official car park.

Moving further north into Penn Road beyond the garden of the Railway Hotel in 1910, the parade of shops, broken only by the entrance to Warwick Road, continues into the distance as a line of houses. Facing the shops, but hidden behind the tree, were a few well-spaced houses.

Also published in 1910, this card shows in detail the two shops on either side of Warwick Road, which then led nowhere, as development had yet to start beyond the visible buildings. Arthur Cheale of London End in the old town had just opened his second drapery shop on the left-hand corner, with the large ironmongery store of the South Bucks Hardware Company on the other side.

Looking south along the shopping parade again in about 1910; it was the width of the road, the shops set well back behind a strip of rough ground which later accommodated a service road, that gave rise to its alternative name, The Broadway. The first shop was Flemons bakery & tea rooms, with R.W. Brooke, 'dispensing and analytical chemist', next door. The third shop was Robarts' model dairy, which boasted 'all milk supplied direct from Grange Farm Beaconsfield, in every way an ideal dairy farm and beyond comparison in the neighbourhood'.

After the First World War, Howard Coad replaced Cheales in 'Warwick House', and this close-up of the display windows also claims it to be, 'The Nicest Shop in Bucks – and the Most Up-to-Date', and, 'The shop that sets the pace and cuts the price!'. This advertisement featured in the town guide.

By 1914, the service road had been constructed in front of the shops and the parade extended northwards incorporating the terraced houses, to which shop fronts had been added. The first of these can be seen at the left of the picture, separated from the original shops by a narrow passage. The sign on Frost's building on the far side of the railway can still be clearly seen from this distance.

Looking north again, the full line of converted houses can be seen beyond the original parade on this 1920 postcard. At the far end of the terrace the last house remained unchanged for several more years, with two more houses between it and the Ledborough Lane turning. The Austin Seven stands outside the last of the original shops, an antique furniture dealers, and beyond it a horse-drawn delivery van of the G.W. & G.C. Joint Railway is standing in the service road.

WHEN IN BEACONSFIELD

You'll Enjoy your Meals at

FLEMONS' TEA and LUNCHEON LOUNGE

The service is prompt and courteous, and most important of all, the Viands are the best procurable and excellently prepared.

Proprietor—

J. KENNETH FLEMONS,

Pastrycook and Confectioner,

6, BROADWAY BEACONSFIELD

Near the Station.

The most comfortable and modern Public Room in the District.

Evening hire of the Lounge can be arranged

Telephone No 70. Telegrams : Flemons, Beaconsfield

In 1925 J. Kenneth Flemons, pastry-cook and confectioner, advertised his 'Tea and Luncheon Lounge' at No. 6 Broadway. This picture shows the interior with its potted palms and well-spaced tables with Lloyd Loom chairs.

In this late twenties view from outside Barclays Bank, the Westminster Bank now has a well-screened garden on its Penn Road side. Next door just beyond it was then a small garage, and then gabled houses beyond that, which had already gained shop fronts. On the other side of the road, the Railway Hotel's sign stands in front of the mature trees in their garden with two petrol pumps alongside

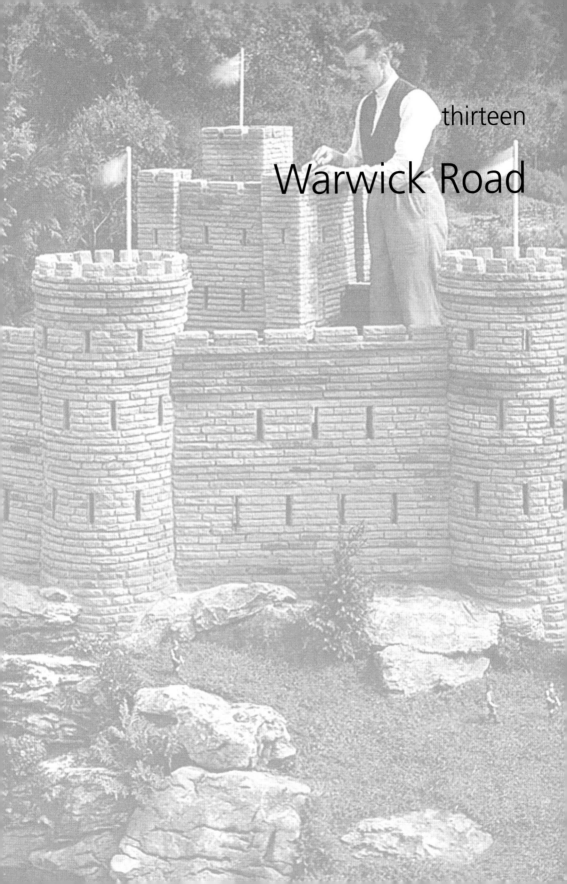

thirteen

Warwick Road

Inside St Teresa's church, the 1939 extension included this chapel, dedicated to the English Martyrs, as a memorial to G.K. Chesterton who had died at his Beaconsfield home three years earlier. The chapel is a representation of a cell in the Tower of London, entered under a drawn-up portcullis. Later additions to the chapel included a memorial to those parishioners who died in the Second World War.

Opposite above: Warwick Road runs from Broadway in Penn Road to the two principal churches of Beaconsfield new town, or Beaconsfield Station, as the area was called when building first started. This view along Warwick Road from just past the shops dates from about 1930, with the recently built Catholic church visible over the hedge on the right and the new Anglican church at the far end of the avenue of chestnut trees. Also in Warwick Road is the recently opened Bekonscot Model Village, on the left beyond the parked car.

Opposite below: Beaconsfield's Catholic church, dedicated to St Teresa, is closely connected with G.K. Chesterton. He was part of the section of the community who initially worshipped in the assembly hall of the Railway Hotel, until the construction of this fine building, which was opened by the Bishop of Northampton in 1927. This picture was taken after the addition of the tower and extension of the nominal 'West End' in 1939. Due to the limitations of the site, the church could not be built with the normal east–west orientation, and so the 'West End' actually faces north.

Opposite the Catholic church is Beaconsfield's most famous attraction, Bekonscot Model Village, which grew out of the joint hobbies (gardening and model railways) of a local man, Roland Callingham, who owned the land, and a friend from Ascot. Initially simply a rock garden with trains, development of the model village began in earnest in 1926, taking its name from a combination of the two men's hometowns. This photograph dates from before it was named, when construction was incomplete, and the miniature trees and shrubs had not matured.

Although the main construction work for the model village was completed by 1930, building maintenance, repairs and repainting have continued ever since, just as in any full-size building. A limited amount of 'modernisation' has been carried out, just like in a real village trying to keep up with the times. In this view, a stone mason is working on the parapet of one of the towers of Wychwood Castle.

Above left: Unofficially at first, visitors and onlookers were welcomed for a voluntary donation to a charity box. Then in 1929, Bekonscot, the first Model Village in the world, opened officially, with admission on a more formal footing. Children paid sixpence (2p) and adults a shilling (5p), for charity. In April 1934 Queen Mary brought her granddaughter Princess Elizabeth to the village as a treat on her eighth birthday. *Above right*: Royal visits became a regular feature during the thirties; in 1936 Princess Elizabeth was accompanied by her younger sister, Margaret Rose. In this picture, taken by Beaconsfield dentist C. Wendell Bleby, the two princesses are standing among the horses taking part in the Bekonscot hunt, an area out of bounds to the general public. After the publicity given to these visits the former trickle of visitors became a regular stream, raising healthy sums for charity, amounting to well over a million pounds in the seventy-four years it has now been open.

After the war, visitor numbers increased considerably and it soon became necessary to introduce a designated 'one-way' system along the narrow pathways, allowing visitors to pass all the main features without too much congestion. Here, on a busy summer's day in about 1950, people were queuing along one of the main paths, held up by those enjoying the view from the footbridge. In the fifties the popular children's writer Enid Blyton, who lived in Beaconsfield, wrote 'The Enchanted Village' for a souvenir booklet about Bekonscot village and railway.

Facing the end of Warwick Road, The Church of St Michael and All Angels stands behind the green of Church Square. New Town's parish church was dedicated in 1916, before housing development had reached that part of the area, and was initially separated by open fields from the new houses of Ledborough Lane in the distance on this 1917 card.

St MICHAELS CHURCH. BEACONSFIELD.

The church soon gained a neighbour, the Parsonage, included in this 1920 photograph, and within a few years it was surrounded by new houses, with only the grass square in front of the church maintained as an open space.

fourteen

Ledborough Lane

Ledborough Lane, Beaconsfield,

Ledborough Lane is one of the original roads of Beaconsfield, linking Penn Road with the main road to Amersham. Development started in the fields on the north side of the lane soon after the arrival of the railway, and by 1910 a couple of dozen large houses had been built on extensive plots on one side for the first half mile from Penn Road, pictured here in 1912. In the next twelve years the fields behind them were filled with similar residences and the other side of the lane had also been built up throughout its length.

Opposite above and below: In the mid-twenties, Miss Warr opened High March kindergarten school in one of the houses in Ledborough Lane. Expanded in the forties to include an upper school, it then gave preparatory education to boys and girls up to the ages of eight and thirteen respectively. A set of postcards was published soon afterwards showing different aspects of the school life, and from this set the upper card is of the kindergarten with children on a climbing frame in the garden, and the lower depicts the handcraft room of the upper school with a mixed group engaged in fretwork and other practical pastimes.

High March
Beaconsfield
The Kindergarten from
The Gard[...]

High March
Beaconsfield
Hand Work Room.

Further along the lane, Ledborough Woods initially prevented building on the north side. In this view of the lane, published in about 1915, the corner of the wood is to the right of the road, with the entrance to Wilton Road to the left of the island.

LEDBOROUGH WOODS BEACONSFIELD.

Ledborough Wood, or Ludborough on early maps, was outside the Urban District boundary, and, until the mid-nineteenth century had been actually outside Buckinghamshire, in a detached area of Hertfordshire centred on Coleshill. This ancient track, just inside the edge of the wood, is still a right of way towards Coleshill, although this corner of the wood has now given way to a road named simply Ledborough Wood.

Above and below: Oakdene school started life in a house of that name in Reynolds Road, advertising in 1910 as 'Beaconsfield High-Class School for Girls', and noting 'The aim of the school is to provide a thorough education on modern methods. Special attention is given to Nature Study, Handicrafts, and Physical Education'. By 1920 it had moved into impressive new premises specially built on a fourteen-acre site off Ledborough Lane, approached by a formal drive from Wilton Road, with full boarding facilities and a separate school chapel. The upper view is of the front of the main building, and the lower, part of the grounds behind the school.

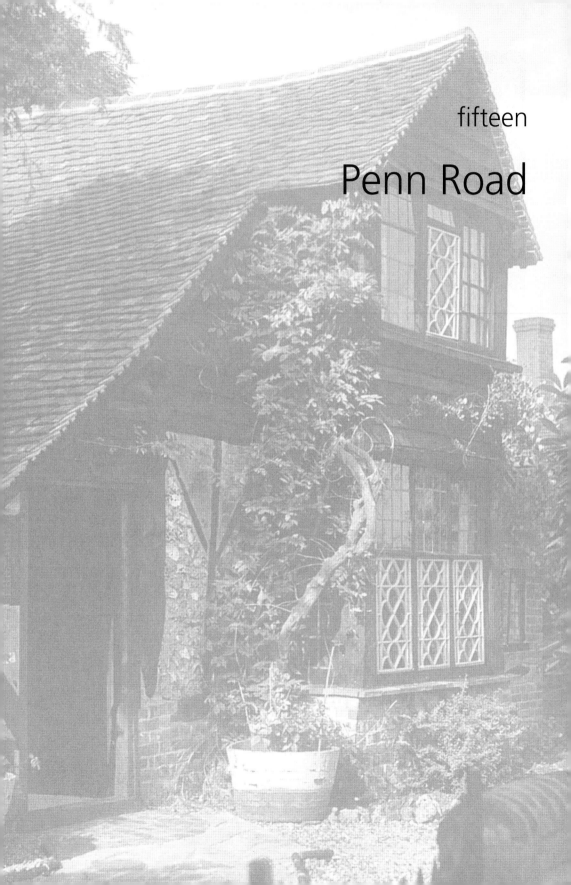

fifteen

Penn Road

For the next half mile beyond the shops, Penn Road formed the eastern boundary of the land belonging to Seeleys Farm. As with most of the existing roads in the area, it was one of the first to be built up and by the twenties the edge of the farmland was lined with more large houses, but the farm buildings and twenty-five acres of orchard close to them remained untouched until after the Second World War. Now only the sixteenth-century farmhouse, pictured in 1915, remains, surrounded by houses.

Beyond the farmland Penn Road continues through the hamlet of Knotty (formerly Knocklocks or Knottocks) Green, with the old Red Lion Inn by the roadside. The inn, pictured in 1910, is built on a sloping site, with its side to the narrow road, which climbs towards Penn Village. Approached by twin flights of steps to the front door, the Red Lion dispensed the popular local ales from Weller's Amersham Brewery.

Knotty Green, which in the eighteenth century consisted of just a few buildings around a village green, started to grow soon after the opening of the railway with an influx of wealthy businessmen who built superior houses on very extensive plots, so that a writer as late as 1930 noted that, 'at Knotty Green the houses are mostly large, with a good deal of land attached, so that the character of the surrounding country has not been unduly interfered with'. This picture, dating from 1912, includes some of the first new houses there.

Beaconsfield Cricket Club, established in 1825, the oldest in the county, usually plays at Wilton Park, but this team photograph was posed after a match played at Knotty Green on 22 July 1922, where 'a crowd of 200 sat down for tea' in the marquee. The players were, from left to right, standing: W. Bates (umpire), E. Bates, G. Perkind, ? Wheeler, ? Wailes, Vincent Jones, ? Webb, ? Robbins, Major Wynyard (umpire), and seated: E. Eggleton, A. Bates, ? Forrester, F. Hancock, ? Mead Taylor, J. Burgess, E. Busby, H. Canvin, A. Child, ? Pinchard.

Right and below: A turning from Knotty Green leads to the smaller hamlet of Forty Green, which still consists of only a handful of houses, but with a world-famous inn, The Royal Standard of England. Among woods and orchards in an area of quiet country lanes in the depth of the countryside, it is of part thirteenth-century, part seventeenth-century origin. Originally called Ye Ship, it was honoured by King Charles II with its present unique title in 1660 after it had served as a Royalist headquarters during the Civil War. The two postcards, from a set published by the inn in about 1950, show part of the exterior and the lounge, which features an ancient ship's settle.